Founding father. John F. Brown.
BROWN BROTHERS
Milawa
VINEYARD AUSTRALIA

Entwined
When wine and food are in perfect harmony

Wine
and food

PASSION. Wine and food are a passion for the Brown family and have been for as long as I can remember. Many of my childhood memories are of the family and extended family getting together to share good wine, food and company. My father is a great raconteur and these gatherings have always had another most important ingredient - laughter! It has given my brothers and I, and the generations that followed, an indelible passion for wine and food and the lifestyle it brings.

Today, wine and food styles have changed, as has the way we entertain. Cultural diversity has given us viticultural and culinary richness. We are enjoying a far greater variety of wine styles and cuisines. There is a greater choice of restaurants and a multitude of ingredients from which to choose.

For my family, wine and food and the richness of lifestyle it brings is a passion that has seen us open our Epicurean Centre. Here, we strive to perfect the art of matching wine and food. This book brings you a few of the recipes that have been prepared by our Epicurean chefs, so that you can enjoy the experience of creating the dishes and then savouring them, over a glass or two.

Ross Brown

IT RUNS IN THE FAMILY. The story of Brown Brothers began with my grandfather, John Francis Brown, who had dreams of owning a family vineyard. In 1885, he set forth to plant his first vines. Four years later, his dream bore fruit when he savoured his first vintage from his modest four hectares.

In 1934, he was joined by my father, John Charles Brown. Anything but a conservative winemaker, my father was one of the first winemakers to recognise the potential of the land at Milawa and it was in these early years that the experiments with different grape varieties began.

By 1956, my parents had four sons who grew to share their passion and eventually joined the business. Today, three generations are involved, making Brown Brothers one of the oldest family-owned and managed wineries in Australia.

A MYRIAD OF VINEYARDS. An infinity of wine styles. The growing of vines has never been easy - weather and pests have all had their effects on the vineyards in the past. Over the last thirty years climate and soil have been the predominant criteria for the selection of Brown Brothers vineyard sites.

TODAY OUR VINEYARDS are as varied as the wines and wine styles we produce. Within a short radius of Milawa lies a range of climatic conditions, from cool alpine highlands to lush temperate valleys to sun drenched plains. It is because of the diversity of the vineyards, which are as cool as Germany and the Champagne region of France or as warm as Spain, that we can produce such an impressive range of premium wines. As each grape has its particular idiosyncrasies, such climatic diversity enables specific sites to be pinpointed for each variety and wine style. The range of climatic conditions is one of the main reasons why we harvest more than 45 different grape varieties each vintage.

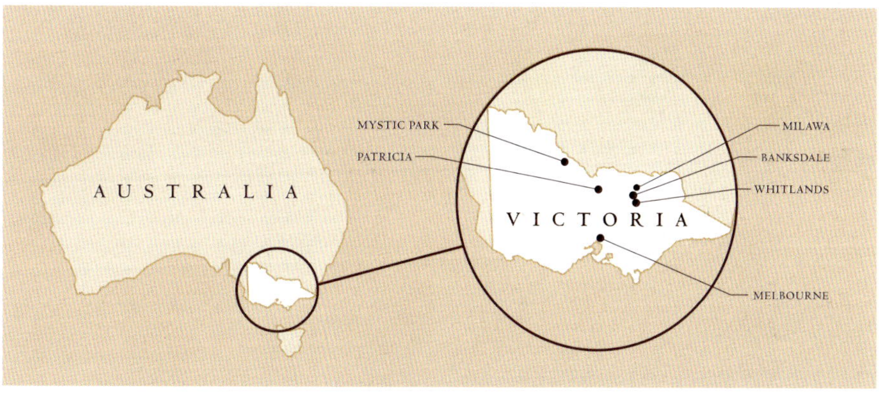

EPICUREAN EXPERIENCE. The Brown Brothers Epicurean Centre is located at the picturesque Milawa vineyard in north-east Victoria, Australia. Here, every dish is created to balance and blend with the flavour and texture of the wine and its 'weight in the mouth'. Often prepared with a contemporary Asian or Mediterranean accent, the frequently changing menu makes a feature of fresh, seasonal ingredients. Each wine is carefully matched with each dish, so that the flavours of the food and wine are enhanced.

RESEARCH AND DEVELOPMENT. Also located at Milawa is our mini winery, affectionately called the 'Kindergarten Winery', which was established to explore and experiment with all facets of the winemaking process. It is where young ideas with great potential are nurtured. The 'Kindergarten Winery' enables our winemakers to experiment with small batch ferments, to trial new grape varieties and fruit from new vineyards, as well as conduct research on viticultural and winemaking practices. Today, many of these innovative wines are widely available - wines such as Barbera, Merlot, Tarrango and Orange Muscat & Flora. Wines that are perfect partners to the recipes in this book.

Whites

BROWN BROTHERS
Chenin Blanc

RIESLING. A deeply flavoured wine with aromas and flavours of lime and lemon blossom with a hint of spice. On the palate, it is delicate with soft citrus flavours, balanced acidity and a long, crisp, elegant finish. Exuberant when young, graceful and poised when aged. Serve lightly chilled.

INGREDIENTS

Serves 8

Pastry
500g plain flour
250g unsalted chilled butter in cubes
chilled water

Filling
60g butter
1kg sliced brown onions
3 medium size eggs - beaten
60g gruyere cheese - grated
salt, pepper to taste
½ teaspoon nutmeg

BAKED ONION AND GRUYERE CHEESE TART (PICTURED)

To make pastry, place flour and butter in a food processor and use the pulse action to make rough crumbs. Add sufficient water to form a dough. Wrap in plastic wrap and refrigerate for 30 minutes. Roll out pastry and fit into a 30cm removable base tin. Refrigerate for 20 minutes.

To make the filling, place butter and onions in a frypan over medium heat and cook for 10 minutes or until golden. Place onions in a bowl and mix with eggs, gruyere and seasoning. Add filling to pastry base and bake tart in a preheated 180°C oven for 20-30 minutes or until filling and pastry are golden. Serve with a leaf salad.

The delicate texture and richness of the tart is balanced by the refreshing acidity and subtle citrus flavours of the Riesling, while the crisp, dry finish of the wine is a perfect foil for the sweetness of the caramalised onions.

INGREDIENTS

Serves 8

8 x 150-180g steaks of fresh water salmon
8 plants of tatsoi or other Asian green salad vegetable (or baby spinach leaves, salad leaves or mixed lettuce)
300g packet dried egg noodles
1 level teaspoon dried wasabi
80ml vegetable oil
150ml Japanese soy

Lemon Vinaigrette
rind and juice of 1 lemon
30ml white wine vinegar
80ml vegetable oil

VICTORIAN BAKED SALMON

Mix oil and wasabi to taste and brush on salmon steaks. Add some more wasabi to lemon vinaigrette for dressing. Soak noodles in boiling water or boil until soft. Wash tatsoi and break from stem. Arrange tatsoi leaves on plate. Bake brushed salmon slices in a preheated oven at 190°C for 8 minutes. Sauté drained noodles in hot wok and then add soy and toss. Arrange noodles on tatsoi leaves. Place baked sliced salmon on noodles. Dress with wasabi lemon vinaigrette. Garnish with spring onion curl or more of the salad greens.

The soft citrus flavours and crisp dry finish of this stylish Riesling balance the zesty flavours of the wasabi oil and lemon, while the palate weight of the wine is in balance with the texture of the salmon.

CHENIN BLANC. Mouth-filling with a clean, crisp acid finish. A white wine reminiscent of summer; of luscious honeydew melon, mango and fresh passionfruit. The natural grape sugars provide roundness and palate weight to this fruity wine. Serve lightly chilled.

INGREDIENTS

Serves 8
(makes 16 fish cakes)

750g white fish fillets (firm flesh - ling, cod etc) skin and bones removed
4 teaspoons red curry paste
2½ tablespoons fish sauce
3 tablespoons cornflour
2 medium size eggs - beaten
2 teaspoons finely chopped red chilli
2 tablespoons chopped spring onion
½ cup finely sliced green beans
oil for frying

SPICY FISH CAKES (PICTURED)

A characteristic of these fish cakes is their firm texture.

Cut the fish into small pieces and process in a food processor until smooth. Add curry paste, fish sauce, cornflour and egg and process until combined. Place mixture into a bowl and stir through chilli, spring onion and beans. Divide mixture into 16 portions, roll each portion into a ball and flatten. Shallow fry the cakes in hot oil until golden brown on both sides and cooked through (5 minutes total cooking time). Drain on absorbent paper. Serve the fish cakes with sweet chilli sauce or a cucumber salad.

Chenin Blanc is a delicious accompaniment to this dish. The fresh tropical flavours and mouth-feel of the wine match the texture of the fish cakes, while the crisp acid finish is a foil for the spice of the red curry paste.

INGREDIENTS

Serves 8

75g butter
75g flour
2½ lts vegetable stock
1¼ kg parsnips peeled and diced
2 pears cored and peeled
2 onions peeled and diced
salt, pepper to taste
bouquet garni
(thyme, bayleaves, parsley)
300ml single cream
150ml basil pesto

CREAM OF PARSNIP AND PEAR SOUP WITH BASIL PESTO

Melt butter and sweat vegetables and add flour to absorb butter. Add vegetable stock and bouquet garni and bring to boil. Simmer, stirring occasionally for one hour. Add pears and simmer for another ½ hour. Remove bouquet garni, puree and strain. Add cream, re-heat (making sure not to boil or cream will curdle) and garnish with basil pesto (1 dessertspoon per bowl).

Chenin Blanc has the palate weight to balance the creamy texture of the soup, while the acidity of the wine cuts through the richness of the soup and the pesto.

DRY MUSCAT. A distinctive dry white wine with an enticing grapey, spicy nose that is full of aromas evocative of musk and tropical fruit. These delicious aromas are echoed on the palate, which is balanced by a refreshing, crisp finish. Serve lightly chilled.

INGREDIENTS

Serves 8

Barbecue recipe
8 butterfly pork loin steaks
2 tablespoons grated fresh ginger
2 tablespoons grain mustard
4 tablespoons Brown Brothers Dry Muscat
sprig fresh thyme - leaves only
salt, pepper to taste
pinch of Chinese 5-spice
160ml olive oil

Mango Salsa
4 medium mangoes, peeled and sliced
4 medium red onions
peeled and thinly sliced
4 spring onions, sliced
120ml sherry vinegar
4 teaspoons sugar

GINGER AND MUSTARD PORK WITH MANGO SALSA (PICTURED)

Combine ginger, mustard, Dry Muscat, thyme, salt, pepper, Chinese 5-spice and oil in large bowl; add pork, mix well. Marinate in refrigerator for at least 3 hours or overnight. Drain pork, discard marinade. Cook on heated, oiled barbecue until browned both sides and cooked to your liking.

Combine mango salsa ingredients and serve with pork and green salad.

The spicy characters of the Dry Muscat are beautiful with the spices used in this dish and the inherently fruity style of the wine partners with the pungent flavour of the mango.

INGREDIENTS

Serves 6

1kg fish fillets (white flesh fish - sole, whiting etc.)
5 medium size egg whites
150ml single cream
300g dry egg noodles
or 500g fresh egg noodles
1 ½ lts fish stock
3 teaspoons red curry paste
salt, pepper, chives, dill to taste

Garnish
1 red pepper
cut into fine strips
8 spring onions
cut into fine strips

ASIAN FISH QUENELLES WITH NOODLES

Puree fish fillets in food processor. Add egg whites, salt, pepper, chives and dill and process until smooth. Continue to puree, gradually adding cream to form mousseline. Mould mousseline into 18 quenelles (egg shapes made by moulding food between two dessertspoons or similar). Steam until firm or poach in simmering fish stock until floating. Bring stock to boil, add red curry paste and simmer. Adjust for seasoning and curry flavour and strain. Prepare noodles as directed on packet and strain.

To serve, heat garnish in stock. Place noodles in base of bowl. Arrange 3 quenelles on each plate. Pour over hot stock and garnish.

The mouth-feel of the Dry Muscat is perfect with the texture of the fish quenelles and noodles, while the spice flavours of the wine link to the hint of red curry paste in the dish.

Reds

BROWN BROTHERS

TARRANGO. A delicious, lively light-bodied red wine with flavours of cherry and raspberry, hints of spice and a dry, crisp finish. This fresh, exuberant wine is best savoured lightly chilled.

INGREDIENTS

Serves 8

Barbecue recipe
1 tablespoon olive oil
1 tablespoon balsamic vinegar
¼ teaspoon coarse ground black pepper
8 tuna steaks

Salad
4 medium tomatoes, chopped
300g pitted black olives
100g roasted and peeled red pepper strips
⅓ cup fresh oregano leaves
2 tablespoons roasted pinenuts

PEPPERED TUNA STEAKS WITH TOMATO AND OLIVE SALAD (PICTURED)

Combine oil, vinegar and black pepper and brush over tuna. Cook tuna on heated, oiled barbecue; brushing occasionally with oil mixture until sealed on both sides. To make the salad, combine all ingredients in a bowl and serve with tuna steaks.

The clean lively berry flavours and hint of spice of Tarrango are simply delicious with the tomato and roasted red peppers and black pepper coating on the tuna. The palate weight of the wine balances with the texture of the tuna steak.

INGREDIENTS

Serves 8

3 red peppers, roasted, seeded and peeled
40 to 48 asparagus spears
100ml olive oil
1 lemon, juiced
500g goats cheese cut into eight slices

GRILLED ASPARAGUS WITH GOATS CHEESE

Reserve one sliced and roasted pepper for garnish. Place remaining red peppers in a blender and puree, then strain through a course sieve. Trim the asparagus, blanch in boiling water until bright green; drain and toss in oil and lemon juice. Warm sauce of pureed red peppers in a small saucepan over medium heat. Barbecue or grill the asparagus until warm and charred. To serve place red pepper sauce on serving plate, top with cooked asparagus, goats cheese and slices of the red pepper.

The refreshing acid finish of Tarrango is the perfect foil for the acidity and texture of the goats cheese while the berry flavours of the wine enhance the sweetness of the roasted red peppers.

BARBERA. An elegant, versatile, medium-bodied red wine with delicate berry aromas and flavours along with a delightful peppery complexity, hint of licorice and a whisper of oak. It is a delicious wine with refreshing acidity and soft tannin finish. Serve at room temperature.

INGREDIENTS

Serves 8

1½ kg loin of pork fully trimmed
16 small new potatoes
6 parsnips cut into 7mm thick circles
4 pears peeled, cored and sliced into 6 wedges lengthways
200g fresh snow pea shoots or tendrils
150ml olive oil

Dressing

3 star anise - crushed
6 blackcurrants
½ teaspoon sesame oil
30ml pomegranate molasses (or red currant jelly or honey)
pinch of black pepper
¾ teaspoon Chinese 5-spice
300ml olive oil
130ml red wine vinegar

CANTONESE FLAVOURED PORK (PICTURED)

Slice the pork into 24 slices and flatten with a meat mallet. Process the dressing ingredients together and marinate pork in half of the dressing overnight. Partly boil the potatoes until just undercooked. Pre-roast the parsnip circles and the pear wedges in some more of the dressing and oil. These need to be just cooked also. Seal and fry the marinated pork in a pan by adding sufficient dressing and oil to moisten the pan and cook until tender. At the same time, reheat the potatoes, parsnip and pear in some of the oil and dressing. Serve potatoes, parsnips and pear on the plate. Top with the sliced cooked pork and garnish with the snow pea shoots (alternatively, use shredded lettuce, Chinese cabbage or bean shoots).

The savoury style of Barbera with its delicate berry aromas and flavours, hint of pepper, licorice and subtle oak makes this wine a delightful partner to the earthy flavours of the root vegetables. While the spices of the dressing find the perfect balance in the spicy flavours of the wine.

INGREDIENTS

Serves 8

8 chicken legs (remove thigh bones but keep all intact)
20 calamata olives
16 prunes - pitted
100ml olive oil
2 teaspoons dried mixed herbs (or substitute fresh herbs if available - basil, thyme)
150ml red wine vinegar
1 tablespoon cracked black peppercorns
4 cloves garlic (cut in half)
8 bayleaves
100g soft brown sugar
1 sprig of rosemary
500ml red wine

Chicken risotto recipe and ingredients below

CHICKEN IN OLIVE AND PRUNE SAUCE

Place all ingredients in a casserole dish or deep roasting pan (can be prepared 2-3 days in advance). Cover with lid or foil. Bake in preheated oven at 180°C for 30 minutes, then remove lid and bake for a further 30 minutes. To serve, place a large spoon of risotto onto the plate, put one piece of chicken on top and roughly divide up the prunes, olives etc. Drizzle plenty of sauce all over. Serve with a bowl of salad.

Chicken risotto for 8 serves, 1½ cups arborio or long grain rice, 3 cups chicken stock, 50ml olive oil, 1 onion cut into 5 mm dice. Simmer chicken stock. In a separate larger saucepan, warm the oil and sauté onion until golden. Add rice and mix well with onion and oil. Stir through a portion of chicken stock until absorbed. Continue to add portions of stock, stirring through until absorbed and all stock is used and rice is tender. Approx. 15 min cooking time.

The gentle tannins of Barbera make it an ideal accompaniment to the delicate texture and flavour of the chicken and the spice flavours of the wine are a fine partner to the prunes, olives, spices and herbs.

MERLOT. A beautiful medium-bodied red wine with soft, delicate, ripe berry fruit flavours along with hints of subtle oak. The wine has crisp balancing acidity, and a mellow, lingering finish with soft silky tannins. Serve at room temperature.

INGREDIENTS

Serves 8

1 ½ kg minced lamb
2 onions, peeled and finely chopped
12 garlic cloves, peeled
and very finely diced
2 medium size eggs - lightly beaten
1 tablespoon oil
1 cup fresh breadcrumbs - soaked
in ½ cup of water for 30 minutes
1 teaspoon each of dried oregano,
marjoram, rosemary
1 teaspoon black pepper
2 teaspoons salt
100ml olive oil
400g salad leaves

Honey yoghurt
250ml yoghurt
100ml honey
2 teaspoons seeded mustard
1 teaspoon chopped rosemary

8 portions flatbread

BARBECUED LAMB WITH HONEY HERB YOGHURT (PICTURED)

Sauté onion and garlic in oil, add the herbs and the soaked breadcrumbs. Cool, add the lamb mince and egg. Divide mix into 8 portions and mould into thick sausages. Rosemary skewers may be used. Cook on a hot barbecue or in a hot frypan until browned and cooked through.

To make the honey yoghurt, combine all four ingredients. Serve the lamb with grilled flatbread, salad leaves and the honey yoghurt.

The sweetness and texture of the minced lamb balance beautifully with the fragrant berry flavours and soft tannins of the Merlot, while the barbecue flavours meld with the smoky oak characters of the wine.

INGREDIENTS

Serves 8

2kg minced pork
10 rashers bacon
300g chicken livers
3 medium size eggs
1 teaspoon salt
1 teaspoon pepper
1 teaspoon nutmeg
1 teaspoon oregano
1 dessertspoon hot mustard
100ml brandy

Spiced quince jelly
200g quince jelly
(or red currant jelly)
2 teaspoons seed mustard
50ml red wine vinegar

PORK AND CHICKEN LIVER TERRINE

Trim livers and marinate in brandy for a few hours. Seal 20 livers in hot pan and hold. De-glaze pan with remaining brandy. Puree remaining livers and add to pork mince with eggs and spices. Line a 26cm cake tin with cling wrap and bacon overlapping to cover base when filled. Add the meat mix to tin and half fill - arrange sautéed livers and fill to top with remaining pork mix. Steam for 1½ hours in pressure steamer or in a water bath in the oven, covered with foil for two hours at 160°C. Let cool, press under weights and refrigerate overnight. Slice chilled terrine, garnish with winter salad of vegetables - witloaf, watercress and spiced quince jelly (made by warming above ingredients together).

The natural red berry fruit and the soft tannins of the Merlot match the texture of the terrine and the richness of the liver. The red berry flavours are in harmony with the quince jelly served with the dish.

SHIRAZ A medium-bodied cool climate red wine that shows aromas and flavours of plum, subtle black pepper and all-spice along with well integrated oak, balanced acidity and fine tannin finish. Serve at room temperature.

INGREDIENTS

Serves 8

1½kg beef fillet, trimmed
150ml olive oil
1 dessertspoon of
cracked black pepper
1 teaspoon oregano
1 teaspoon tarragon
8 slices of potato
100mm x 25mm thick
cut from large potatoes
(1½-2kg total potato)
3 tablespoons tomato paste
3 bay leaves
500ml beef stock
with 8 juniper berries
200g beans
1 Spanish onion diced in 5mm
200g semi-sun dried tomatoes
cut in half lengthwise

PEPPERED BEEF (PICTURED)

Marinate beef in oil, pepper and herbs overnight or for at least four hours. Preheat oven to 200°C. Roast potato slices in a little of the beef marinade for 45 minutes. Seal beef in a hot fry pan and then roast for 8 to 10 minutes at 200°C. Into the fry pan, add the tomato paste, bay leaves and the beef stock and simmer to reduce to a sauce. Remove the beef from the oven and allow it to rest in a warm place before slicing. Blanch the beans and slice into 2cm lengths. Mix the diced onions, sliced beans and sliced semi-sun dried tomatoes together. Strain the sauce created in frypan and keep warm.

Place sliced beef onto the roasted potato slices, sprinkle the vegetable mix around the plate, pour warm sauce over and serve. Garnish with a sprig of fresh herbs.

The succulence of the beef, natural sweetness of the vegetables interwoven with the aromatic juniper berries and black pepper are in perfect harmony with the pepper, all-spice and oak flavours of our Shiraz.

INGREDIENTS

Serves 8
(makes 16 curry puffs)

4 sheets ready prepared puff pastry cut into quarters
1 medium size egg-beaten

Filling
1 dessertspoon red curry paste
1 teaspoon ground tumeric
30ml vegetable oil
8 chicken thigh fillets, diced into 1cm pieces or 800g diced chicken meat
2 medium carrots
2 medium potatoes
1 small celeriac or 2 sticks of celery
½ cup water

Dipping Sauce
400ml ready made eggplant dip - add half teaspoon cracked black pepper

CHICKEN AND VEGETABLE CURRY PUFFS

Filling: Place curry, tumeric and oil in a frypan and cook for 1 minute over high heat. Add chicken and cook for 5 minutes. Add finely chopped vegetables and water and cook for 5 minutes until water is reduced. Allow to cool.

To assemble: Divide filling in equal portions in the centre of the pastry quarter. Brush the edge with beaten egg and fold over. Decorate the edges in a rope roll or with a fork. Deep fry at 160-170°C in cotton seed oil or similar until golden and drain on absorbent paper. Serve with the eggplant dipping sauce and Asian style salad (blanched bok choy, tatsoi, mibuna, mizuna etc).

The hearty flavours of this dish provide a flavour explosion and as such require a wine to match. Our Shiraz with its delightful flavours of pepper, all-spice and oak, harmonise with the aromatic and exotic ingredients of the curry puff and dipping sauce, while the soft tannins counter the richness of the pastry.

Stickies

BROWN BROTHERS
HARVESTED
Orange Muscat
and Flora
VICTORIA

LATE HARVESTED ORANGE MUSCAT & FLORA A luscious wine that exudes wonderful aromas of ripe muscat, fragrant orange blossom, mandarin and a hint of tangy citrus. These succulent fruit aromas literally 'burst in the mouth' and linger on the palate with mouth-filling satisfaction. Serve lightly chilled.

INGREDIENTS

Serves 8-10

600ml single cream
1 vanilla bean, bruised
4-6 medium size egg yolks
100g caster sugar

500g strawberries, cleaned & halved
250g caster sugar
300ml boiled water
rind of one orange
juice of 2 lemons

STRAWBERRIES AND VANILLA BEAN CREAM (PICTURED)

Heat cream with vanilla bean until almost boiling, remove from heat and allow to stand for 1 hour. Remove vanilla bean. Mix yolks and sugar in a heatproof bowl over a saucepan of simmering water. Pour on scalded cream and stir until mixture has thickened enough to coat the back of a wooden spoon. Strain immediately. Ladle into individual 80mm soufflé dishes and refrigerate for 4 hours or overnight.

To marinate the strawberries, place sugar and water in a saucepan and stir over low heat until dissolved. Add rind and lemon juice to pan and allow to cool. Stir strawberries into cold syrup and serve with the vanilla bean cream.

The hint of orange blossom in the Late Harvested Orange Muscat & Flora highlights the citrus flavours of the accompanying syrup, whilst the zesty finish is perfect with the natural acidity of the strawberries.

INGREDIENTS

Serves 6-8

Sauce
2 medium size navel oranges
100g caster sugar
250ml water
3 tablespoons maple syrup

Pudding
100g softened unsalted butter
100g caster sugar
2 tablespoons maple syrup
2 medium size eggs
100g self-raising flour

Garnish
300ml double cream

ORANGE AND MAPLE STEAMED PUDDING

To make sauce, cut one of the oranges into slices about 4mm thick. Put the sugar and water into a frying pan and bring to a gentle simmer, stirring to dissolve the sugar. Poach the orange slices for 5 minutes. Remove with a slotted spoon and drain on paper towels. Grease a 1 litre heatproof pudding basin and arrange the slices over the base and sides. Pour the maple syrup over the slices.

To make pudding, cream the butter, sugar and maple syrup until pale and creamy. Add the finely grated zest of the second orange. Beat in the eggs and fold through the flour. Spoon into the lined basin and cover with greased foil (or non-stick baking paper), pleating it in the middle (to allow room for the pudding to expand). Tie the cover securely with string and place on an upturned saucer in a large pan. Fill the pan one-thirds full with boiling water and simmer over medium heat for 1½ hours topping up with water from time to time. Remove from pan and turn pudding on to a warm serving platter. Garnish with cream and orange maple syrup sauce. Tip: if you prefer, the oranges can be peeled before lining the bowl, in which case there is no need to cook them first.

The succulent orange and mandarin flavours of the Late Harvested Orange Muscat & Flora are in harmony with the orange syrup, while the refreshing finish of the wine counteracts the richness of the maple syrup.

LATE HARVESTED MUSCAT. This wine has delicious fragrant, musky aromas that are echoed on the palate, which is mouth-filling and nicely balanced by a clean acid finish. Serve lightly chilled.

INGREDIENTS

Serves 12

300g self-raising flour
300g sugar
60g poppyseeds
12g lemon zest
90ml milk
6 medium size eggs
360g butter, melted

Lemon Syrup Glaze
175g sugar
150ml lemon juice
300ml pure cream

SWEET LEMON AND POPPYSEED CAKE (PICTURED)

Combine flour, sugar, poppyseeds and zest in a bowl. In another bowl mix milk and eggs. Add butter and ½ milk mixture into dry ingredients. Mix on low to moisten - beat for one minute. Gradually add rest of egg mixture in two additions. Bake 175°C for 15 minutes in greased 125ml dariole moulds or muffin tins, or in a 22cm round spring form tin for 1 hour.

To make the lemon syrup glaze, combine sugar and lemon juice and place over low heat until sugar has dissolved. Pour hot syrup over hot cake and allow to cool slightly before serving with cream.

The fragrant, fruity flavours of the Late Harvested Muscat enhance the citrus component of the dish, while the delicate, fresh style of this wine suits the light, delicate texture of the cake.

INGREDIENTS

Serves 8

500g fresh mascarpone
500g fresh seedless grapes
400ml sugar syrup (200ml water simmered with 200g caster sugar to dissolve - cool - add juice of ½ lemon)

Tuille

140g caster sugar
90g butter
85g sifted flour
90g ground roasted hazelnuts
3 medium size egg whites - lightly beaten

MASCARPONE AND TUILLES

Make the tuilles in advance and store in an air tight container: Melt butter and caster sugar together. Add the sifted flour and the ground hazelnuts and stir. Add the egg whites and stir in to form a paste. Spread this mixture out onto silicon or baking paper into rounds of 6cm diameter x 3mm thick. Bake for 10 to 15 minutes at 160°C until golden. Repeat to use all the mixture. Cool on wire racks.

Wash and de-stem the grapes and place into sugar syrup for 1 hour. Scoop the mascarpone onto plates and arrange the marinated grapes. Serve with tuilles placed into mascarpone or separately. Garnish with sprigs of fresh mint.

The Late Harvested Muscat picks-up the sweetness of the grapes whilst enhancing the nutty flavours of the tuilles. The palate weight of the Late Harvested Muscat is also in harmony with the texture of the mascarpone.

LIQUEUR MUSCAT The combination of muscat fruit, quality spirit, judicious blending and long oak ageing, gives this magnificent dessert wine a lasting impression. The intense (balanced) raisin flavour reflects the care taken to bring this wine to its peak. Serve at room temperature.

INGREDIENTS

Serves 8

Pudding
125g soft butter
125g caster sugar
1 medium size egg - beaten
½ teaspoon vanilla essence
50g cocoa
200g sifted self-raising flour
200g ground roasted hazelnuts
125ml Liqueur Muscat

Sauce
200g dark chocolate
50ml water
50g brown sugar
100ml Liqueur Muscat

CHOCOLATE AND MUSCAT PUDDING (PICTURED)

To make pudding, cream together butter and sugar. Add egg and vanilla. Mix sifted cocoa, self-raising flour and ground roasted hazelnuts together. Add the dry ingredients (one third at a time) to the butter, sugar, egg and vanilla mixture, alternating additions with the Muscat. Mould into 8 greased 125ml dariole moulds. Place in a water bath covered with foil and steam for 1 hour at 180°C. To make sauce, warm all ingredients together, stirring to dissolve to make a smooth rich sauce. Garnish with rich cream and perhaps some shaved chocolate.

The addition of the ground roasted hazelnuts to the pudding provides balance and symmetry and is the link between the palate weight of the Liqueur Muscat and the texture of the pudding. The intense raisin flavour of the Liqueur Muscat also marries beautifully with the delectable sauce of dark chocolate and muscat.

INGREDIENTS

Serves 8

250g dark chocolate
3 tablespoons water
125g butter
3 medium size eggs - separated
100g icing sugar - sifted
1 teaspoon vanilla essence

Sugar Syrup
100g brown sugar
100ml boiling water
25ml Liqueur Muscat

Garnish
rich cream or
crisp hazlenut biscuits
and grapes or
dried muscatels in sugar syrup

RICH CHOCOLATE TIMBALE

Melt the chocolate with the water in a bowl over a saucepan of hot water. When melted, remove from the heat. Beat the butter until creamy. Beat the yolks one at a time into the butter with the icing sugar, vanilla and cooled chocolate mixture. Beat egg whites until stiff peaks form and then fold through the chocolate mixture and pour into a greased 600ml fluted mould or 125ml individual dariole moulds. Place in refrigerator overnight or until set.

To make syrup, place brown sugar and water in a bowl and stir until sugar has dissolved. Stir through Liqueur Muscat and serve with rich cream or crisp hazelnut biscuits and grapes or dried muscatels in sugar syrup.

The Liqueur Muscat with its intense richness, raisin flavours and complexity is one of the few wines that can stand up to the intensity and richness of this rich chocolate concoction.

Sharing

We hope you have enjoyed using Entwined - Wine & Food by Brown Brothers. If you would like to receive more information about Brown Brothers, please return this reply card. Alternatively, write to us at the address overleaf and we will be delighted to help.

☐ Please send details of Brown Brothers Tastings/Wine and Food events in my area.

☐ Please send details of where I can purchase Brown Brothers wines locally.

☐ Please send information about visiting Brown Brothers Cellar Door and Epicurean Centre in Australia.

☐ Other information - Please specify:

____

____

Title: Mr ☐ Mrs ☐ Miss ☐ Ms ☐

First name:____________________ Surname:____________________

Address:____________________________________

______________________________ Postcode:__________

Home telephone number:______________________________

Affix
stamp

Brown Brothers Wines
PO Box 1491
MAIDENHEAD
SL6 8GS